Unveiled

God's Heart for His People

Participant's Workbook

Susan Lanford

New Hope® Publishers
P.O. Box 12065
Birmingham, AL 35202-2065
www.newhopepubl.com

© 2000 by New Hope® Publishers
All rights reserved. First printing 2000
Printed in the United States.

No part of this publication may be reproduced, stored in a retrieval system, or transmitted in any form or by any means (electronic, mechanical, photocopying, recording, or otherwise) without the prior written permission of the publisher.

Dewey Decimal Classification: 220.07
Subject Headings: Bible-Study and Teaching
  God (Christianity)
  Spiritual Life

Cover illustration by Art Roper

N004142•1100•5M1

Introduction

Welcome to the beginning of eight pivotal weeks in your life—eight weeks on a journey taking you closer to the heart of God than you've likely been in a long time.

Unveiled is quite an appropriate title for this book and the video series that accompanies it. When Moses received the Ten Commandments from God on Mount Sinai and then returned to address the Israelites, his face was radiant from being in the presence of God. As the radiance faded, we learn from Exodus 34:33, Moses put a veil over his face so that God's people could not see that the radiance was leaving him. But when he next went into God's presence, "he removed the veil until he came out" (Ex. 34:34). When the Israelites saw the veil, they knew they were hearing the words of a man; when Moses came to them "unveiled," they knew they were hearing the voice of God.

Paul contrasted his ministry of the gospel of Jesus Christ with Moses' ministry to the Israelites so many years earlier. Paul said that for those trying to live by the old covenant alone, "a veil covers their hearts" (2 Cor. 3:15). But the new covenant of Jesus Christ means "the veil is taken away" (2 Cor. 3:16).

Unveiled! We are like the Israelites of Moses' day and the Jewish believers of Paul's day—relying on our human understanding of God's purposes for His people—unless we are willing for those purposes to be unveiled.

Paul concluded the beautiful third chapter of 2 Corinthians with these words:

> "And we, who with unveiled faces all reflect the Lord's glory, are being transformed into his likeness with ever-increasing glory, which comes from the Lord, who is the Spirit" (v. 18).

And this is the invitation you've been extended through this study, the invitation:
1. for God's heart to be unveiled to you,
2. for you to offer Him your willing obedience to His purposes for His people, and
3. for you to continue the process of re-creation, being transformed into the likeness of the Savior you so love.

Prepare yourself for a wide range of responses to *Unveiled*. This is spiritually humbling stuff, because you'll be brought face to face with some narrow, incomplete interpretations of Scripture you've held. This is also spiritually heady stuff, because you'll feel your spirit invigorated by the winds of truth—complete truth.

Meet Bob Sjogren

Bob is your video host and Bible teacher on each of the videotapes in the *Unveiled* series. Bob describes himself this way: "I am a mobilizer, a professional agitator. My goal is to make Christians uncomfortable!" Your discomfort will produce an interior spiritual agitation; but if you're willing, it will also mobilize you in ways that reinvigorate your life and its purpose as one of God's children.

Bob's teaching will lead through panoramic theological ideas. At the same time, he'll offer you practical, doable actions that bring those ideas back down to earth.

Accept Bob's basic premise—that we must view the Bible as one book, with one story, and one theme—and you're ready to begin this series. Bob challenges us:

> "We must align our lives, families, and churches with what God has been doing for 4,000 years. This material has a proven track record of altering long-term goals and plans and dreams. It is only for those who are serious about obeying what God reveals to them."

Participating in an Unveiled Study

Please consider these suggestions as your *Unveiled* study begins:

1. Open your calendar; block off the eight study sessions, and do not let anything keep you from 100 percent attendance. The session materials which follow in this book are useless to you unless you have viewed the video. All the exercises, prayer times, and responses assume that you've watched each session's video segment.

2. Arrive on time for each session. Thirty minutes is spent viewing the session's video. Your group will probably have 15-30 additional minutes in which to debrief your spiritual insights and struggles from the previous week and to begin discussing the current session's material. Time will move very quickly, so don't miss a minute of it!

3. Enlist prayer support from a wise, mature Christian during these eight weeks. Remember, Bob intends to agitate your Christian comfort zone. Even if you manage to hold the impact of these sessions at bay, you will still have an unsettled, almost queasy feeling in your soul. You need someone interceding for you, petitioning God for the strength, insight, and will to be obedient to all you will learn from God's Word. This person will celebrate with you the new freedom you experience in obedience.

Format of This Book

Because of the prominence of videotapes and VCR's in this experience, you'll find each session's material in this book labeled with the following video terminology:

PAUSE

This section is to be completed prior to the session. It offers time to reflect (hence, the "pause") and pray based on the material you've just studied. Sometimes your responses will become part of a prayer experience during the group session itself. Take time to complete PAUSE before each session.

REWIND

This section is a brief review of the previous session's key ideas. Because the sessions build on one another, it is important to review where you've just been in order to travel the next leg of the journey. Take time to complete REWIND before each session.

RECORD

This section is your listening sheet for taking notes of the video segment. The intention is to help you focus on Bob's key points and write them down as he says them. Some of you may find it more distracting than helpful; if so, fill in the blanks ahead of the session and let your eyes follow the completed notes as you listen (the answers for the blanks are provided at the end of each session's material). This section captures the essence of each videotape and provides you with a full set of notes you'd have difficulty making if you started from scratch.

REPEAT

This next section includes additional information from the video and is used as a discussion starter in your group.

POWER

This section provides a variety of journaling experiences to follow up on each session. Sometimes the journaling will require only a few minutes. Sometimes, as in session 3, you're asked to do a journaling exercise on four different days. Why is this called POWER? Because this is where you truly interact with the Scriptural challenges Bob issues in the videotapes and with the Spirit's leadership in your life to grow and change based on those challenges. Next to seeing the videotapes themselves, this section is the most important one in making this study full and meaningful to you. This portion is where the spiritual water hits the wheel.

Occasionally you may be asked to share some of your journals to offer a key insight you've gained; but, the journaling experience is almost exclusively yours. There are no right answers that everyone in the group will strive to record. What you record is right if you've been honest, confessional, and humble before God in the process. Give yourself the time to revel in your journal each week, and you will give yourself a rich and precious gift. In the process, you may then be able to offer back to God "a living sacrifice, holy and acceptable to Him."

Father, we want to give back to You the veil
behind which we hide from Your truth.
We ask for the courage to step into
the brightness of Your radiant light and
to be Your enthusiastic, obedient followers
to the ends of the earth.
For the sake of Your kingdom, Lord.
Amen.

SESSION 1

The Story of the Bible

PAUSE

Reflect for a moment:
1. What did it take to get you here?

2. Why do you think you came?

Record an insight you've gained from these two questions about your motivation for coming. Then identify the obstacles you will have to overcome to complete this study.

Write a prayer confessing to God the obstacles that may tempt you during this study and keep it from being a life-changing experience for you. Then include a prayer of thanksgiving that He has provided enough motivation for you to start and can help you complete what He has begun today.

REWIND

Not counting Sunday School, in how many Bible studies have you participated during your Christian life? _____
Why do you join Bible study groups?

Based on all your Bible study to date, how would you complete this sentence: The best way to study the Bible is

Indicate whether you agree or disagree with this statement: The Bible is too diverse to have only one theme. Agree/Disagree

Explain your answer:
_____
_____

RECORD ──────────────────────────────

I. Introduction

A. Most Christians are __clueless__ about the Bible.

B. The best way to study the Bible is as __one__ book with __one__ story having __one__ theme.

SESSION 1

II. The Bible is one book with an introduction, the main story, and a conclusion.

A. The Bible's introduction is found in __Genesis__. The introduction culminates in Genesis 11 where the people did not have an "__Us-Them__ mentality." They wanted equality with the only "them" there was: __God__. God saw two problems:

1. God saw their pride. Some of the Scriptural phrases that point to their pride: "Come _____ _____"
"_____ may make"
"a name for __ourselves__."

2. God saw that with __one__ language, Satan could mislead them all with __one__ lie. When God divided the languages among them, it was an act of __mercy__.

B. The Bible's story is found in __Gen 12:2,3__.

1. The pivotal passage which introduces the Bible's story is God's choosing of Abram, because it introduces us to the two essential threads of the Bible: the __top__ __line__ of the covenant and the __bottom__ __line__ of the covenant.

   The top line of the covenant refers to __blessings__.
   The bottom line of the covenant refers to __responsibilities__
   _____.

2. The key word, *peoples*, can be translated as:
   F __amilies__
   T __ongues__
   T __ribes__
   E __thnic__ G __roups__
   P __eople__ G __roup__

The worst translation of *peoples* is: _____

Session 1

3. Genesis __12:2,3__ is the beginning of the Bible's Great Commission theme.

4. Does Jesus understand the Abrahamic covenant as being the foundational starting passage for the Scriptures? We find an answer in ____Matthew 28____.

   Ps 67:1

   Jesus confirms the two central themes of the Scriptures when He says:
   a. "The Christ will suffer and will rise from the dead on the third day" (v. 46). This means:
   ____Power over death, forgiveness of sins____

   This refers to the (circle one) **top**/bottom line of the covenant.

   b. repentance and forgiveness of sins will be preached in his name to all nations" (v. 46). This means:
   _____

   This refers to the (circle one) top/**bottom** line of the covenant.

   c. Jesus proved the __Great__ __Commission__ theme from the (circle one) **Old**/New Testament.

C. The Bible's conclusion is found in _____.

   1. Revelation 5:9 teaches us that what God set out to do __in the beginning of the Bible__ He pulls off at __the end of time__.

   2. "If you take _____ out of the Bible, you'd have _____ _____ _____ to study.

REPEAT _____

Charting the Covenant

Translated as:	Found in:
love, righteous obedience, if we fear him his covenants are kept	Ps 25:10,14 Ps 103:17-18 Ps 111:5,9 Jer 11:2-4

POWER

1. Explore the top line of the covenant in your life. List the blessings God has given you in the following categories. Make your list carefully and prayerfully.

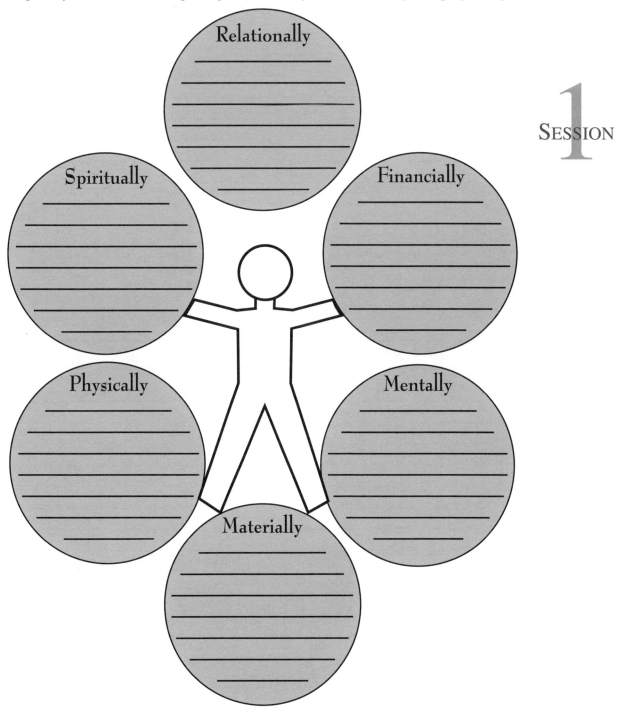

SESSION 1

2. Choose one uninterrupted hour this week for reading the accounts of the covenant made with Abraham. Use the spaces that follow to write your insights and responses to each passage. Consider using a translation of the Bible that you do not typically read to help you view these stories in a new, fresh way.

The Story of the Bible

SESSION 1

Genesis 12:1-9

Genesis 17:1-8

Genesis 22:1-19

Session 1

The Story of the Bible

Answers for the blanks

SESSION

I. Introduction:
  A. clueless
  B. one; one; one

II. The Bible is one book with an introduction, the main story, and a conclusion.

  A. Genesis 1-11; us-them; God
   1. "Come let us"; "we may make"; "a name for ourselves"
   2. one; one; mercy

  B. Genesis 12-Jude
   1. top line; bottom line
      the blessings God wants to give us; the responsibilities we have to be a blessing to the "thems" of the world.
   2. Families; Tongues; Tribes; Ethnic Groups; People Groups; Nations
   3. 12:2-3
   4. Luke 24:45-48
      a. The blessing God wants to give us comes through Christ; top.
      b. Our responsibility to all the people of the world; bottom. Great Commission; Old

  C. Revelation
   1. In the beginning of the Bible; the end of time
   2. missions; very little else

Session 2

The Creative Covenant Communicator

PAUSE

Review the motivations for beginning this study that you identified as you started session 1. Did your experience with session 1 and your preparation for this session change your motivations? In what ways?

_____
_____

Review the obstacles you also identified as you started session 1—obstacles that will interfere with or interrupt your commitment and participation. What impact did these obstacles have on you as you prepared for session 2, if any?

_____
_____

Pause to find a favorite Scripture that helps protect your motivation to be changed by this study and addresses the obstacles you face. Write the Scripture below.

_____
_____
_____

Use the words of the Scripture to make your prayer.

REWIND

Session 1 revolved around this key proposition: The Bible is one book with one story having one theme. Review some key ideas from session 1 by filling in these blanks again:

The story has three main parts, corresponding to three sections of Scripture. List the three parts and the corresponding Scripture references:

1. _____   _____
2. _____   _____
3. _____   _____

Respond to the following key ideas from session 1 by marking the phrase that best describes your reaction to each one:

1. Thinking of the Bible as a book with one story and one theme:
   _____ a. upsets every notion I've held about the Bible.
   _____ b. is something I've never considered as possible before now.
   _____ c. seems to discount the complexity and variety of the Bible's history, key truths, and characters.

_____ d. is something I'm willing to explore and consider.
_____ e. is already bringing changes in my spiritual life.

2. Being told that "Christians are clueless about the Bible" is such a strong statement. Do you prefer the phrase "clueless about"? If not, which of the following phrases would you prefer to fill its place:
_____ a. devoted to
_____ b. not grateful enough for
_____ c. too focused on fighting with one another about
_____ d. neglectful to consistently study

3. The concept of a top line and a bottom line to God's covenant:
_____ a. was a novel concept to me
_____ b. makes perfect sense to me
_____ c. pushes me to study Scripture in an entirely new way
_____ d. prompts me to call a wiser Christian than I and discuss this idea more
_____ e. is going to change my life, isn't it?

RECORD

I. Special emphasis in the Old Testament on the covenant with Abraham

A. Abraham's son is to be sacrificed on the altar   True or false?
   Genesis 22:16-18 contains the top and bottom lines of the covenant.
   This is the _____ time the covenant promise was made to Abraham.
   This time, God swears "_____ _____."

B. God repeats the covenant five times:
   _____ time(s) to Abraham
   _____ time(s) to Isaac
   _____ time(s) to Jacob

   What is happening?

C. God is using _____ as an _____ device.

II. Examples of the covenant woven throughout the entire Bible:

A. The _____ Land
   1. Top line of the covenant: _____
   2. Bottom line of the covenant: The Promised Land was _____ _____ in the midst of all the _____, according to Ezekiel 5:5.
B. The calling to be _____ is seen in two ways:

1. Specific calling of the _____ to minister to the eleven other tribes.
2. General calling of the _____ to all the nations. "You will be for me a _____ of _____," according to Exodus 19:6.

C. Great Commission theme in the Old Testament:
1. God gave the Great Commission theme to the _____, Abraham's _____ descendants.
2. Jesus crystallized it in the Great Commission to the _____, Abraham's _____ descendants.

III. Understanding Matthew 28:18-20

A. The four action verbs in this passage are:
G_____
M_____ D_____
B_____
T_____

The main verb of the four is: M_____ D_____

B. How do you make disciples of all nations?
1. Baptize—Water baptism means putting your _____ on the line, identifying with _____.
2. Teach—Go to every distinct _____ _____ on the face of the earth and start a church.

C. In Matthew 24:14, Jesus says that the gospel will be preached to _____ _____ and then the _____ will come.

Why is God so concerned with reaching all nations first before the end comes?
1. If God didn't reach all the nations, He would have _____ a _____ to Abraham, and God would be called a _____ for all eternity.

2. God gets greater glory when He _____ that which is diverse. His greatest glory is when _____ _____ are brought together in harmony by His Son.

The Creative Covenant Communicator

REPEAT _____

Find the following Scriptures, mentioned in this session's tape. List the words which follow the word *all* or refer to the non-Jewish world in each Scripture.

1 Chronicles 16:23-24— _____
Psalm 72:11— _____
Isaiah 60:1-3— _____
Jeremiah 3:17— _____
Daniel 7:14— _____
Malachi 1:5, 11— _____

SESSION POWER _____

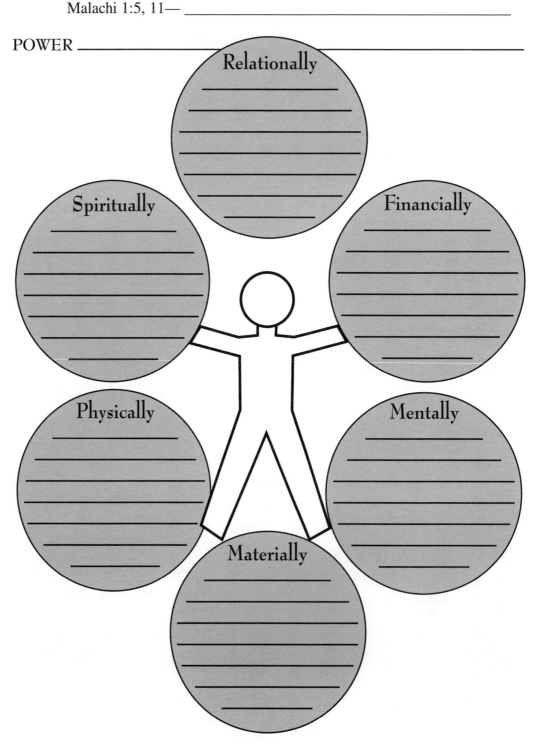

16

1. Explore the bottom line of the covenant in your life. Based on the lists of blessings you generated after session 1, how have you seen God's name made known to all the nations through your blessings? Make your list carefully and prayerfully in the circles on page 16.
2. Choose one uninterrupted hour this week to remember truths about God's love that you have sung. Think of lyrics in favorite choruses or Scriptures set to music that exalt God's love. If possible, look up favorite hymns in a hymnal. Play tapes or CDs of songs praising God for His love. Use part of your hour to sing your praise to God.

Then record several phrases or lyric lines that are most meaningful to you. In your journal write your thoughts, insights, and prayers to God regarding His love.

SESSION

Session 2

Answers for the blanks

I. Special emphasis in the Old Testament on the covenant with Abraham

A. True; third; "by myself"
B. 3; 1; 1
C. repetition; attention-focusing

II. Examples of the covenant woven throughout the entire Bible

A. Promised
 1. a blessing given by God to His chosen people
 2. centrally located; nations
B. priests
 1. Levites
 2. Jews; kingdom; priests
C.
 1. Israelites; physical
 2. church; spiritual

III. Understanding Matthew 28:18-20

A. Go; Make Disciples; Baptize; Teach; Make Disciples
B.
 1. life; Christ
 2. ethnic group
C. all nations; end
 1. broken; promise; liar
 2. unifies; all nations

SESSION 3
A Simple Equation for God's Plan

PAUSE

Review your journal based on hymns and songs about God's love. Choose three truths about God's love that this journaling experience reminded you of and list them here:

1. _____
2. _____
3. _____

In the margin beside each truth above, note whether it is a top line or bottom line expression of God's love. Then, record your emotional reaction to those notes, perhaps joyful, indifferent, ashamed, angry, pleased, or some other feeling:
_____.

Review your list of top line blessings from session 1 found in the POWER section of your workbook. Then record your emotional reaction to the top line blessings you listed; perhaps joyful, indifferent, ashamed, angry, pleased, or some other feeling:
_____.

Review your list of bottom line blessings from session 2 found in the POWER section of your workbook. Then record your emotional reaction to the top line blessings you listed, perhaps joyful, indifferent, ashamed, angry, pleased, or some other feeling:
_____.

After the time of directed prayer led by your facilitator, describe your prayer experience:
_____
_____
_____

(text of the directed prayer is in the leader's guide)

REWIND

Review some key ideas from session 2 by filling in these blanks again:

1. God repeated the covenant made with Abraham three times, found in these Genesis passages:

   _____   _____   _____

20

A Simple Equation for God's Plan

2. The four action verbs in Matthew 28:18-20, the Great Commission passage, are:
   G_____
   M_____ D_____
   B_____
   T_____
   Circle the most important of those four verbs.

3. God gets greater glory when He _____ that which is diverse. His greatest glory is when _____ _____ are brought together in harmony by His Son.

Session 3

RECORD

I. Top line (A) + bottom line (B) = God's promise to Abraham (C)

A. Doing the Math:
   1. If A>B, then God has a greater desire to bless the _____ than the rest of _____.
   2. If A<B, then God has a greater desire to bless the _____ than the _____. This is not a possibility because of the message of Scripture.
   3. A=B is the only possible equation because God loved the _____ as much as He loved all the _____ of the earth.

B. Checking the Scriptures:
   1. Deuteronomy 7:6 says, "God chose _____ out of all people on the earth." Sounds like A ___ B.
   2. Deuteronomy 18:4-5 describes how God chose the _____ tribe out of all the other tribes of Israel because He had a special _____ for them to do.
   3. Applying this insight to Deut. 7:6, does God choosing Israel mean that God loved the Israelites more? No, it means God had a special _____ for the Israelites. They were a _____ because they were to _____ to all the people coming through Israel.

C. This truth for today: Most Christians are living an A ___ B life. Why?

D. The test of Psalm 46:10. Finish the verse: "Be still and _____ _____." This is the _____ line of the covenant. But most of us don't know the rest of the verse which is the _____ line of the covenant.

E. For most Christians, reading the Bible is like _____ at a _____, being caught up in a "_____ _____" that wants to know, "Where am _____ in the Bible?"

SESSION 3

II. A=B examples from Sunday School stories

A. Moses and the ten plagues:
1. The top line we typically emphasize: _____
2. The bottom line we typically miss: The plagues knocked down the _____ of the _____. God does major things in the world to bring people to _____.
3. Today's application: _____ through the _____.

B. Command to observe the law:
1. Top line we typically emphasize: _____
2. Bottom line we typically miss: _____
3. Today's application: Cast your _____ so that Christ will be _____ among the _____.

C. Solomon and his riches:
1. The top line we typically emphasize: _____
2. The bottom line we typically miss: The whole world sought him out. God blesses _____ and _____ for a reason.
3. Today's application: Our technology and resources bring the _____ to _____.

III. A=B emphasized in Scripture
(Jot down the main idea in the following Scriptures quoted on the tape.)

A. Theological truth:
1. Numbers 15:15: _____
2. Exodus 12:48-49: _____
3. Leviticus 24:15-16: _____
4. Leviticus 24:21-22: _____

B. Practical truth:
1. Amos 9:7: _____
2. Zechariah 2:10-11: _____
3. Exodus 6:6-7: _____
4. Exodus 7:4-5: _____
5. Ezekiel 25:1-5: _____

WHY? BECAUSE A ___ B!

REPEAT

In the tape, Bob administered his Psalm 46:10 test. Try to recall the entire verse and write it below. If you are stumped, work together as a group to reconstruct the entire verse before checking in your Bibles,

"Be still, and . . .

_____

_____

_____."

Write the reference for your A=B verse to memorize: _____

Describe your reason for choosing it:

_____

_____

POWER

Bob provides powerful, practical applications of familiar Bible stories. This week, choose four days and reserve at least 30 minutes on each of those days to explore these applications and to journal your feelings, questions, and responses. You've come this far in this challenging, turn-your-world-upside-down study. Please don't skimp on these exercises but continue the process of change and growth in your life and spirit.

SESSION 3

Session 3

Day 1: Daniel in the Lion's Den

1. Read Daniel 6. Read it as if it had just happened in some world capital.

2. Describe how you feel emotionally and spiritually after reading the story.

3. What questions are you left with after reading this chapter? What else do you wish you knew about this incident?

4. The application Bob offers is this: Get involved with internationals living around you. Finish today's journaling by writing all you know about the ethnic groups living near you and about international people who visit your community. Then list at least three steps you can take to make this application in your life.

Session 3

A Simple Equation for God's Plan

SESSION 3

Day 2: Moses and the Ten Plagues

1. Read Exodus 7-11. Read it as if it had just happened in some world capital.

2. Describe how you feel emotionally and spiritually after reading the saga of the plagues.

3. What questions are you left with after reading these chapters? What else do you wish you knew about these happenings?

4. The application Bob offers is this: God does major things in the world to bring people to Himself, so pray through the news. Pause to browse today's newspaper. Finish your journaling by writing prayers to God about what is happening in at least three faraway places.

A Simple Equation for God's Plan

Day 3: Observing the Old Testament Law

Session 3

1. Read Matthew 15:1-21. Read it as if the confrontation had just occurred within your own church.

   _____

2. Describe how you feel emotionally and spiritually after reading the story.

   _____

3. What questions are you left with after reading this story? What else do you wish you knew about this incident?

   _____

4. The application Bob offers is this: Cast your vote so that God is glorified in the nations. He is advocating for the powerful impact of living out our faith in a way that proves to unbelievers the life-changing power of the gospel. Finish your journaling by recalling the most recent incident at your church in which you were involved where God was not glorified and His gospel was obscured. Write a prayer of confession and contrition about this event. Can you find the courage to call someone who was hurt, angered, or confused by this incident and offer your confession and contrition to them as well?

Session 3

A Simple Equation for God's Plan

Session 3

Day 4: Solomon and His Riches

1. Read 2 Chronicles 1-2,7. Read it as if it had just happened in some world capital.

2. Describe how you feel emotionally and spiritually after reading about Solomon and all the ways he was blessed.

3. What questions are you left with after reading these chapters? What else do you wish you knew about these happenings?

A Simple Equation for God's Plan

4. The application Bob offers is this: Our technology and resources bring the world to us. Once again browse your newspaper, looking for references to various ethnic groups and cultures in your community—perhaps refugees resettled, migrant workers, graduate students, first or second generation naturalized citizens, and so forth. Use your journaling to record ways your paths cross with any of these people or groups. What simple changes could you make to cross their paths more often?

SESSION 3

A Simple Equation for God's Plan

Session 3

Answers for the blanks

I. Top line (A) + bottom line (B) = God's promise to Abraham (C)

   A. Doing the Math:
      1. Israelites; humanity
      2. Gentiles; Israelites
      3. Israelites; peoples
   B. Checking the Scriptures:
      1. Israel; >
      2. Levite; job
      3. Purpose; priesthood; minister
   C. >
   D. know that I am God; top; bottom
   E. looking; yearbook; "yearbook theology"; I

II. A=B examples from Sunday School stories

   A. Moses and the ten plagues:
      1. God wanted to redeem His people out of bondage
      2. gods; Egyptians; Himself
      3. Pray; news
   B. Command to observe the law:
      1. Obey the law and you will be blessed
      2. Our obedience to the law affects how other nations view Christianity
      3. vote; glorified; nations
   C. Solomon and his riches:
      1. Solomon was blessed more than any other man
      2. people; nations
      3. world; us

III. A=B emphasized in Scripture

   A. Theological truth:
      1. Numbers 15:15: Israelites and the aliens were the same before the Lord
      2. Exodus 12:48-49: Same law applies to all
      3. Leviticus 24:15-16: Same law applies to all
      4. Leviticus 24:21-22: Same law applies to all
   B. Practical truth:
      1. Amos 9:7: God treated all the nations equally
      2. Zechariah 2:10-11: Many nations will be called His people
      3. Exodus 6:6-7: Then Israel will know "I am the Lord"
      4. Exodus 7:4-5: Then the Egyptians will know "I am the Lord"
      5. Ezekiel 25:1-5: Then the Ammonites will know "I am the Lord"

   A = B

SESSION 4

Dying with the Blessing

PAUSE

Before the session, review the four days of journaling you did this week. Restate the four applications about which you wrote in your own words:

1. Get involved with internationals living around you.

2. Pray through the news.

3. Cast your vote so that God is glorified in the nations.

4. Our technology and resources bring the world to us.

List the prayer requests generated by your group at the beginning of this session:

REWIND

Match the following equations with their correct meanings:
- ____ a. A>B
- ____ b. A<B
- ____ c. A=B

1. God loves all the nations equally.
2. God loves the Israelites more than the Gentiles.
3. God loves the Gentiles more than the Israelites.

Recall the impact you experienced while listening to Bob describe "yearbook theology" in the session 3 tape. Did you like his terminology and its explanation? Why or why not?

Now browse through one of your school yearbooks. Find yourself again in its pages. Recall your dreams and goals when you finished this school. How much does your life today reflect those former dreams and goals?

Reread the glowing predictions others made about you and your future. Are you the person they predicted you would be? Explain your thoughts.

_____
_____

Plan to bring your yearbook to session 4.

Session 4

RECORD

I. **Jesus' opinion on A (top line covenant promises and blessings) versus B (bottom line covenant responsibilities)**

   A. The job description for the Messiah is found in Isaiah 49:6, indicating God would send an (circle one) A>B; A<B; A=B Messiah to the Jews and Gentiles.

   B. In Matthew 15:21-28, Jesus was with the Canaanite woman. This passage often is used by _____ evangelists because Jesus says to the woman, "I was sent only to the lost sheep of _____" (v. 24).

   Why did He say this?
   1. Matthew 15:1-21 records Jesus' confrontation with the _____ and _____ over the disciples' keeping of the law. After that confrontation, He and the disciples withdrew to a _____ region.
   2. Jesus didn't answer the woman's cry for help because He was waiting for the _____ to respond to the _____ He had just given them. Their response was to _____ _____ _____.
   3. By first ignoring the woman, and then by saying to her, "I was sent only to the lost sheep of Israel," Jesus was living out their _____ to show them what it really was. He had been trying to teach them an (circle one) A>B; A<B; A=B lesson, and they had failed the test.

II. **A=B in practical terms**

   A. The church's _____ have become an end unto themselves. The North American church is dying a _____, _____ death—dying in the _____.
   1. _____ percent growth in North American Caucasian churches. _____ percent of American Protestant churches are either stagnant or dying
   2. What does this mean?
      GOD WILL _____ US EVEN IF IT _____ US.
      GOD IS LOOKING FOR PEOPLE WHO CAN _____ THE _____.

3. _____ is not a thin little paperback book on the shelf called _____. It is the shelf that holds up all the other books.

REPEAT

Record answers to the following information gleaned from your church's current budget:

____ percent of the total given to missions
____ percent of the total given for buildings and maintenance
____ Number of ministries sponsored by the church touching other cultures and ethnic groups
____ Number of church members participating in those ministries to other cultures and ethnic groups
____ percent of the total spent on curricula, books, special events, and other expenditures benefiting church members
____ Number of church members involved in missions experiences outside the borders of the United States

SESSION 4

POWER

Bob strongly believes that most ministries of the church are an end unto themselves, meaning they are designed only to produce top line blessings. He cites the example of the Dead Sea as being "dead" because the water flows into it but never out of it. Take time in your journaling to make an application from these thoughts to the ministries in which you are involved. Record your thoughts about these questions:

1. How do the stated goals or aims of these ministries reflect top line or bottom line results? In the lives of others touched by these ministries?

_____
_____
_____
_____
_____
_____

2. How do your reasons for being involved reflect your focus on top line or bottom line results?

_____
_____
_____
_____
_____
_____
_____

3. If God was allowed to change these ministries so that top line and bottom line results occurred, what do you think He would do?

_____
_____
_____
_____
_____
_____
_____

PLEASE NOTE: This journaling time is not intended to criticize anybody or any ministry. It is intended to help you look at places where you've invested your Christian life and evaluate yourself as much as the ministries themselves in light of what you are learning in this study.

OPTIONAL JOURNALING ACTIVITY

If you have traveled outside the borders of the United States, reflect on those trips and ask God to show you insights through your memories about top line and bottom line examples that you saw. Perhaps you saw cathedrals without congregations; what does that mean to you today? Perhaps you saw crowded marketplaces but no evidence of a Christian witness; what does that mean to you today? Perhaps you saw Christian groups who had no material blessings to speak of, but who possessed an incredible zeal to tell others about Christ; what does that mean to you today?

Answers for the blanks

I. **Jesus' opinion on A (top line covenant promises and blessings) versus B (bottom line covenant responsibilities)**

   A. A=B
   B. Muslim; Israel
      1. Pharisees; Sadducees; Gentile
      2. disciples; teaching; send her away
      3. theology; A=B

II. **A=B in practical terms**

   A. ministries; slow; painless; blessing
      1. 0; 85
      2. BLESS; KILLS; SURVIVE; BLESSING
      3. Missions; Christianity

SESSION 5

A Gracious God and Protective Blindness

PAUSE

List the bottom line ministries for which your group prayed at the end of session 4:

_____
_____
_____
_____

Do you feel God directing you to become involved in any of these bottom line ministries? _____

Would you have to give up something top line in your life to do so? If so, what?
_____

What effects would this change have on your job, your family, or your reputation?
_____
_____

Write a prayer asking God to change the desires of your heart to match His desires and to direct your path to reflect His desires.

_____
_____
_____
_____
_____
_____

Consider memorizing Psalm 37:4 this week.

REWIND

Review some key ideas from session 4 by filling in these blanks:

What distorted ideas have you had about missions or missionaries, even from your childhood?
_____
_____

The Bible is _____ book with _____ story having _____ theme.

In the equation, A+B=C:
A means: _____
B means: _____
C means: _____

RECORD

I. Paul says there is a mystery: Gentiles are a part of the kingdom.
  A. Ephesians. 3:4-6— "A mystery "not made _____ to other _____."

  B. Col. 1:25-27—Two important truths:
   1. Christ is "_____ _____" versus being "with you."
   2. Christ is "_____ _____," and "you" means the Gentiles who were previously not a part of the covenant.

II. God chooses to hide some things so that we may not understand.

Why would God choose to put something in the _____ and not give _____ any _____ into it? Why put the _____ _____ theme in the Old Testament and not _____ it to the _____?

  A. Based on Deuteronomy. 31:16-18, does God know our future disobedience? Yes or No
  B. Based on Ezekiel 20:13-14, God describes Israel's track record of _____, speaking specifically about the _____ _____ incident.
   1. Moses used God's words in Exodus 32:10 to build His case: "a _____ _____," referring to the _____ line of the covenant. Moses' argument is: If God destroys His people, He will never _____ the _____ line of the covenant.
   2. God's response explaining why He spared the Israelites is, "For the sake of my _____." God did what would keep His reputation from being _____ in the eyes of the _____ in whose sight He brought out Israel.

III. Understanding Guilt
  A. Understanding the chart:
    D = _____
    I = _____
    P = _____
    GL = _____
    Blue area = _____
    Outside the blue area= _____

SESSION 5

SESSION 5

B. On the edge of this grace is a _____ _____,
   God's final opportunity offered for our _____ where
   _____ takes place.

C. Two examples about disobedience and insight:
   1. Who had tremendous insight but blew it once? _____
   2. Where was tremendous disobedience but very little insight?
      _____ and _____

D. *NOTE:* Judgment does not refer to _____ or
   _____, but to being taken out of the game called
   _____ prematurely.

E. Guilt is composed of (1) _____ and (2) _____.
   Which is easier for God to limit? _____.

IV. Implications of this teaching on disobedience and insight

A. *NOTE:* God established a stubborn stronghold of _____
   _____ which limited their _____ so that as
   their _____ line was growing, it never crossed out of that
   _____ line of judgment.

B. Description of protective blindness:
   1. Eyes that do not _____
   2. Minds that are _____
   3. _____ hearts
   4. _____ in hearts
   5. "I hid My _____"
   6. _____ of the mind
   7. Minds made _____
   8. A spirit of _____

C. Progression of protective blindness:
   1. We all start out in _____.
   2. God gives us _____.
   3. God reveals Himself to those who are _____. But if He
      sees _____, He allows the protective darkness to remain.

D. What did God blind the Israelites to? The _____ line of the
   covenant because He knew of their future _____. This is
   why Paul says this is a mystery kept _____ for all ages and
   generations.

V. The bottom line revealed again

A. The mystery is now being disclosed because of the _____ of the _____ _____ who makes us more inclined to be _____.

B. God withholds _____, allowing us space and time to _____ and step back toward _____, keeping us from _____.

C. Why? Because He's a _____ God, and He doesn't want us _____ before our time.

REPEAT

- If God had revealed it to the Israelites, then He would have to hold them accountable.
- If God had held them accountable, then He would have to judge them.
- If God had judged them, then He would have ruined His reputation.
- If God had ruined His reputation, then no nation would choose to follow Him.
- If no nation had chosen to follow Him, then He couldn't fulfill the bottom line of the covenant.
- If He could not fulfill the bottom line of the covenant, then He would be a liar for all eternity.
- If He was a liar for all eternity, then He could not receive the greater glory.

POWER

Reflect on times or topics when—as you now understand it—God was limiting your insight. Choose one of those times or topics and describe it.

_____
_____
_____
_____

Look back at the eight descriptive phrases from Scripture used in the video. Which one(s) best describes the experience about which you've just written? Circle at least one:

1. Eyes that do not see
2. Minds that are closed
3. Calloused hearts
4. Hardening in hearts
5. "I hid My face"
6. Confusion of the mind
7. Minds made dull
8. A spirit of stupor

What do you deeply desire to know about that experience now?

_____
_____
_____
_____

Assess your readiness to be obedient to all God is saying to you, especially through this study, by marking an "X" on each of the following lines:

Spiritually ready_____ Spiritually not ready

Emotionally ready_____ Emotionally not ready

Financially ready_____ Financially not ready

Finally, review the four applications from your journal found in the POWER section of session 3. What changes are occurring in your life because of the ideas and plans you wrote about in that session?

1. Getting involved with internationals living around you

_____
_____

2. Praying through the news

_____
_____

3. Recalling the most recent incident at your church in which you were involved where God was not glorified and His gospel was obscured

_____
_____

4. Finding ways your path can cross with any people or groups that the world brings to us because of our resources or technology

_____
_____

Answers for the blanks

A Gracious God and Protective Blindness

SESSION 5

I. **Paul says there is a mystery: Gentiles are a part of the kingdom.**
   A. known; generations
   B.
      1. in you
      2. in you

II. **God chooses to hide some things so that we may not understand.**
   Scripture; anyone; insight; Great Commission; reveal; Jews
   A. Yes
   B. rebellion; golden calf
      1. great nation; top; fulfill; bottom
      2. reputation; profaned; nations

III. **Understanding guilt**
   A. Understanding the chart:
      D = Disobedience
      I = Insight
      P = Patience of God
      GL = Guilt Line
      Blue area = God's desire to show His grace is greater than His hatred of sin
      Outside the blue area = God's desire to show His hatred of sin is greater than His desire to be gracious
   B. dividing line; repentance; judgment
   C.
      1. Moses
      2. Sodom and Gomorrah
   D. *NOTE*: heaven; hell; life
   E. disobedience; insight; insight

IV. **Implications of this teaching on disobedience and insight**
   A. protective darkness; insight; guilt; final
   B.
      1. Eyes that do not see
      2. Minds that are closed
      3. Calloused hearts
      4. Hardening in hearts
      5. "I hid My face"
      6. Confusion of the mind
      7. Minds made dull
      8. A spirit of stupor
   C. Progression of protective blindness;
      1. darkness
      2. insight
      3. obedient; disobedience
   D. bottom; disobedience; hidden

V. **The bottom line revealed again**
   A. power; Holy Spirit; obedient
   B. insight; repent; obedience; judgment
   C. loving; judged

SESSION 6

The Biblical Basis for Spiritual Blindness

PAUSE

Search for some of your favorite verses on prayer. How can the truths you find in them help you pray about the difficult subjects you've encountered in this study? Write the prayer truths and a short prayer for each topic listed:

1. Top line blessings
   Prayer truths (list Scriptural references, too):
   _____
   _____

   How I can pray about this:
   _____
   _____
   _____
   _____

2. Bottom line blessings
   Prayer truths (list Scriptural references, too):
   _____
   _____

   How I can pray about this:
   _____
   _____
   _____
   _____

3. God's judgment for disobedience
   Prayer truths (list Scriptural references, too):
   _____
   _____

   How I can pray about this:
   _____
   _____
   _____
   _____

4. God's protective blindness
   Prayer truths (list Scriptural references, too):
   _____
   _____

   How I can pray about this:
   _____
   _____
   _____
   _____

REWIND

SESSION 6

Review some key ideas from session 5 by filling in these blanks again:

1. God established a stubborn stronghold of _____ _____ which limited the Israelites' _____ so that as their _____ line was growing, it never crossed out of that _____ line of judgment.

2. Progression of protective blindness:
   a. We all start out in _____.
   b. God gives us _____.
   c. God reveals Himself to those who are _____. But if He sees _____, He allows the protective darkness to remain.

3. What did God blind the Israelites to? The _____ line of the covenant because He knew of their future _____. This is why Paul says this (the bottom line of the covenant) is a mystery kept _____ for all ages and generations.

RECORD

I. The graph supported by Scripture
   A. Isaiah 6:1,3. Isaiah said, "I _____ the Lord," a description of _____ insight.
      1. With that insight, Isaiah knew he was going to be _____.
      2. The message of God (in Isaiah 6:9-10) in light of their _____ is protective _____. Otherwise, they would have obeyed the _____ line call and had tremendous _____.
      3. This passage shows that there is a direct relationship between:
         a. disobedience and _____
         b. obedience and _____

   B. Isaiah 29:9-11: "The Lord has brought over you a _____ sleep. He has sealed your _____."

The Biblical Basis for Spiritual Blindness

1. God's vision is "nothing but words _____ in a _____."
2. God won't throw His _____ before swine, because if He did, the disobedient would be held _____ and have to be _____.

C. Isaiah 42:18-20 is a passage describing _____ disobedience; God's Word is difficult to understand among the _____ for the sake of His _____.
   1. Who are we dependent on to gain insight into His Word? _____ _____
   2. Obedience comes before insight. If you're _____ to do God's will, He'll _____ you what it is!
   3. On what basis is God looking at our lives to determine whether or not He's going to give insight into His Word? Our future _____ or _____.

II. Jesus understood protective blindness
   A. Matthew 13 records the Parable of the Sower. When Jesus said:
      1. "knowledge of the secrets of the kingdom of heaven," He meant _____
      2. "you," He meant the _____
      3. "them," He meant other Jews, the _____

   B. Jesus makes His law great and glorious and difficult to _____.
   But, anyone with a heart for obedience will get more _____.

III. Blindness still exists today
   A. Out of God's love for _____, He puts up with _____ in His church.
   B. Out of God's love for people in other _____, He puts up with _____ in the world.

REPEAT _____

Insight
→ Obedience → See God's glory go to all the nations of the earth
→ Disobedience → God may blind you once again

Bob closed the video segment by saying, "May God give us all the wisdom to obey and live out the bottom line so we may see His glory go to all the nations on the face of the earth."

What does wisdom have to do with obedience? Check the following references:
Deuteronomy 4:5-8 _____
Psalm 19:7-11 _____
Psalm 119:98-100 _____
Proverbs 9:10-12 _____
Proverbs 12:1-3 _____
Proverbs 13:10 _____
Matthew 11:19 _____
1 Corinthians 1:25-31 _____
2 Timothy 3:15 _____

POWER

In the session 6 video, Bob asks some crucial questions you need to ask and answer. These three questions will be the basis of your journaling for this week. Enter a season of prayer before you begin writing. Prepare yourself to be honest and confessional as you answer.

1. Have I been blind to the priority of the Great Commission before this series? Explain your answer.

   _____
   _____
   _____
   _____
   _____
   _____
   _____
   _____
   _____
   _____
   _____
   _____
   _____
   _____
   _____
   _____
   _____
   _____
   _____

2. Why is God now giving me these insights into the Great Commission themes of the Scripture?

   _____
   _____
   _____
   _____

Session 6

3. What will happen to me if I have these insights but my life doesn't change?

Answers for the blanks

I. The graph supported by Scripture
  A. saw; high
    1. judged
    2. disobedience; blindness; bottom; insight
    3. blindness; insight
  B. deep; eyes
    1. sealed; scroll
    2. pearls; accountable; judged
  C. high; nations; righteousness
    1. God Himself
    2. willing; show
    3. obedience; disobedience

II. Jesus understood protective blindness
  A.
    1. insight
    2. disciples
    3. disobedient
  B. understand; insight

III. Blindness still exists today
  A. nonbelievers; disobedience
  B. religions; disobedience

Session 7

Old Testament Ties to the Abrahamic Covenant

PAUSE

The journal topics following session 6 may have been difficult or uncomfortable. Reflect on what you wrote, and then choose each response below that best describes how you feel today about those three questions.

1. Have I been blind to the priority of the Great Commission before this series?
   _____ a. I don't mind it that I was blind in the past because my eyes are opening now.
   _____ b. I have been blind, but I didn't recognize my spiritual handicap until now.
   _____ c. I object to the word blindness; that is not the work of a loving God.
   _____ d. I am dealing with regrets over lost opportunities to understand God's Word.
   _____ e. I am dealing with guilt over missed opportunities to tell others about Jesus Christ.

2. Why is God now giving me these insights into the Great Commission themes of the Scripture?
   _____ a. I know why I'd do it if I were God—to shame me.
   _____ b. His timing is perfect; He knew I wouldn't have understood the implications of all this until now.
   _____ c. This is the next logical step in my spiritual growth as a Christian.
   _____ d. My enrolling in this class was accidental; He is using my mistake for His purposes.

3. What will happen to me if I have these insights but my life doesn't change?
   _____ a. I'll be blinded again to God's purpose in my life.
   _____ b. I'll be blinded again to God's purpose in the world.
   _____ c. I'll be merely tolerated by God in my disobedience.
   _____ d. I'll miss the top line blessings because I have not been committed to my bottom line responsibilities.
   _____ e. All of the above.

Before session 7 begins, call your prayer partner assigned during session 6. Talk together about your answers to these three questions. Pray together, confessing honestly your sins, doubts, and fears to God, as well as your praise, gratitude, and joy.

Old Testament Ties to the Abrahamic Covenant

Record below how you feel when this prayer time with your partner concludes:

_____
_____
_____
_____
_____
_____
_____
_____

Session 7

REWIND

Review some key ideas from session 6 by filling in these blanks again:

1. Whom are we dependent on to gain insight into His Word? _____ _____

2. On what basis is God looking at our lives to determine whether or not He's going to give insight into His Word? Our future _____ or _____.

3. Obedience comes before insight. If you're _____ to do God's will, He'll _____ you what it is!

RECORD

I. God gave Abraham the land, but the people couldn't have it for 400 years

A. God needed to preserve the _____ of His people.

B. The incident with the Shechemites over Jacob's daughter, found in Genesis _____, hurt God's reputation. Dangers from that incident:
 1. The Israelites could have _____ their ethnicity
 2. They were _____ God's reputation
 3. They would be _____ _____ as a people.

C. God sent the people for 400 years to _____, found in Exodus 1:8-10, where:
 1. Israel became _____ as a people.
 2. They remained a distinct _____ _____ because as slaves, they never _____.

II. God used the redemption of His people

A. God began a campaign to _____ His reputation, using the ten _____.
 1. Exodus 9:14: God reached out to the _____.
 2. Exodus 9:16: "That My name might be _____ in all the earth."

51

B. Were the nations hearing of this?
1. Exodus 18:1: _____ in Midian heard because _____ had spread God's reputation around the _____.
2. Joshua 2:11: Rahab said to Joshua's spies: "Our hearts _____ because of you."
3. Daniel 9:15: "You who made for yourself a _____ that endures to this day."

SESSION 7

III. The Promised Land

A. Deuteronomy 7:16: God said to _____ all the peoples the LORD your God gives over to you.

B. Deuteronomy 9:4: Because of their _____, God is driving out the people.

C. With God's people executing His judgment, it sounds like A _____ B, but it wasn't.

IV. A king over Israel

A. Israel had _____ kings; then God _____ the kingdom. Why?
1. 1 Kings 11:1-6: Solomon was beginning to _____ other gods in temples at _____ he had built.
2. God began a judgment of Israel, _____ the kingdom so as not to have His _____ completely _____.

B. "Even though we do not see Abraham, Isaac, or Jacob's descendants going out to the _____, we must not assume that this is _____ that God did not want them to go. More likely, we must conclude that this is evidence of their _____ which resulted in _____."

V. Judgment by dispersion among the nations

A. God told _____ to tell the kings of all the earth, "You will serve my _____ Nebuchadnezzar, King of _____."
1. Each king knew: (1) "I have my own _____," and (2) "Nebuchadnezzar doesn't _____ the God of the Israelites."
2. Jeremiah's message was dismissed until they were _____ by Nebuchadnezzar.
3. This re-established God's _____ and judged His _____.

B. Ezekiel 5:11-12 records God's judgment:
⅓ will _____ of plague and famine
⅓ will _____ by the sword
⅓ will _____ among the nations

C. Zechariah 7:13: "I scattered them with a whirlwind among all the
   _____."

D. This is God's "involuntary go mechanism":
   1. "If you won't go, I'll _____ you."
   2. When Israel asked, "Why?" it finally dawned on them they had been _____ and needed to _____. When they did, they were in all the nations, bearing witness to the _____!
   3. Ezekiel 12:14-16: "They will _____ that I am the Lord."
   4. Daniel 3:29: Nebuchadnezzar decreed the _____ of the world!

VI. God called Israel back

A. The walls of Jerusalem were rebuilt in _____ days.
   1. Top line blessing: The walls were rebuilt _____ _____ _____ _____.
   2. Bottom line responsibility: "This city will bring me renown before all the _____ on earth. They will be in _____" (Jer. 33:9).

VII. Esther's story

A. Top line: God protects His _____.

B. Bottom line: Many other nationalities became _____ because fear of the _____ had seized them (Esther 8:17).
   1. Esther set the stage for world _____.
   2. This was repeated in Paul's ministry when he went to the synagogues and addressed "the _____ and the God-fearing _____."

REPEAT _____

Bob exhorts you in this session's video segment: "Look at the major events in your life and integrate the bottom line into them."

Old Testament Ties to the Abrahamic Covenant

List major events from your life in the following categories. You'll recognize the format of this chart from sessions 1 and 2, used in a different way here.

SESSION 7

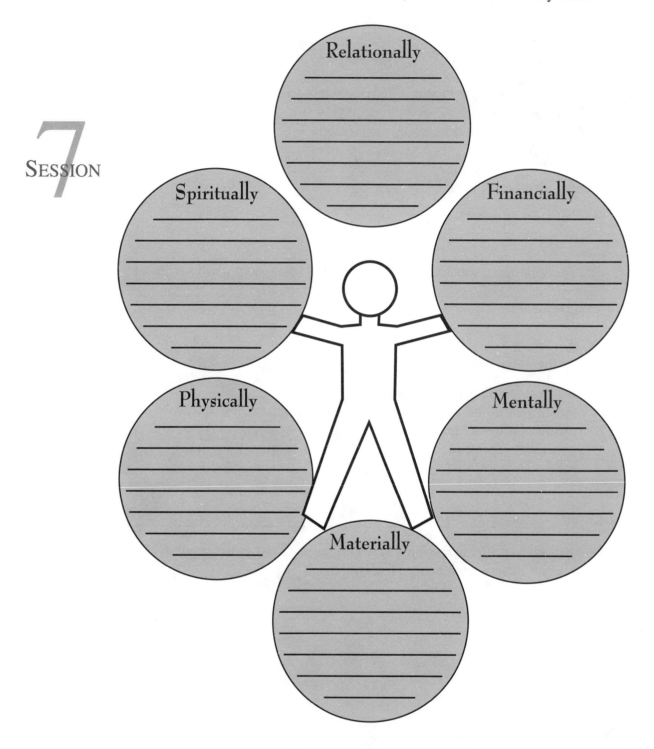

54

POWER

Protect at least one hour this week—two would be better—to do your journaling exercises. They involve your response to a lengthy chapter in the Bible. Choose your time to avoid interruptions. Also, prepare yourself through prayer to be open and honest in God's presence as you examine again a very familiar story.

John 9 records the healing of a man blind from birth and the intense questioning he endured by religious authorities after he regained his sight. Read the entire chapter and then write a description of key persons in the passage. Write these descriptions as if it were a police missing-persons report.

The man blind from birth:
_____
_____

The disciples:
_____
_____

The man's neighbors:
_____
_____

The Pharisees:
_____
_____

The man's parents:
_____
_____

Jesus:
_____
_____

Which of these descriptions most closely describes you today? Explain your answer:
_____
_____
_____
_____

As the story unfolds, you can see the progression of the blind man's faith. He saw Jesus first as a man (v. 11), then as a prophet (v. 17), then as one sent from God (v. 33), and finally as his Lord (v. 38). Reflect on the evidence in your life

SESSION 7

that you are both a top line and bottom line Christian. What does that evidence say about how you see Jesus Christ? Choose one of these four categories, and explain your answer.

_____
_____
_____
_____
_____
_____
_____
_____

Session 7

The healed man responds once to his accusers by saying, "<u>Once</u> I was <u>blind</u>, but now I <u>can</u> <u>see</u>" (v. 25, Williams Version). Rewrite that verse below, substituting words for those underlined, to most accurately reflect your spiritual condition today. (For example, someone might rewrite it: "As a new Christian I was seeing God's purpose clearly, but now I act like I am blind to it.")

_____
_____

Jesus ends this story with the words spoken to the Pharisees in verse 41. His words echo in an almost eerie way all that Bob has been saying about protective blindness. What can you do to ensure that your guilt—over your blindness, your lack of understanding of the Scriptures, or your focus on top line blessings but not bottom line responsibilities—does not remain past today? Write the cry of your heart and soul on this matter, knowing you are in the presence of a watchful, loving, and judging God.

_____
_____
_____
_____
_____
_____
_____
_____
_____
_____
_____
_____
_____
_____
_____
_____

Answers for the blanks

I. God gave Abraham the land but the people couldn't have it for 400 years

A. ethnicity
B. 34:24-25
  1. lost
  2. ruining
  3. wiped out
C. Egypt
  1. numerous
  2. ethnic group; intermarried

II. God used the redemption of His people

A. establish; plagues
  1. Egyptians
  2. proclaimed
B.
  1. Jethro; traders; world
  2. melted
  3. name

III. The Promised Land

A. destroy
B. wickedness
C. >

IV. A king over Israel

A. three; divided
  1. worship; altars
  2. dividing; reputation; ruined
B. Gentiles; evidence; disobedience; judgment

V. Judgment by dispersion among the nations

A. Jeremiah; servant; Babylon
  1. army; serve
  2. defeated
  3. reputation; people
B. die; fall; scatter
C. nations
D.
  1. send
  2. disobedient; repent; Gentiles
  3. know
  4. evangelizing

VI. God called Israel back

A. 52
  1. as they were before
  2. nations; awe

VII. Esther's Story

A. people
B. Jews; Jews
  1. evangelization
  2. Jews; Gentiles

Session 8

New Testament Ties to the Abrahamic Covenant

PAUSE

In this session's video, you'll hear about the day in Jerusalem when Jesus cleared the Temple. We typically associate this incident in Jesus' life with the emotion of anger. We use it to learn principles of anger management. Jesus felt outrage and probably even deep sorrow over practices at the Temple.

Read the story again in Mark 11:15-19. Notice these things as well:

1. He seemed to have a deliberate plan of action "on reaching Jerusalem." Jesus didn't accidentally discover the blatant commercial dealings within the Temple; He undoubtedly knew about them, and knowing His ministry was soon to end, knew He had to give a clear message and offer repentance.

2. Notice that when the commerce stopped and the problem was solved, He began teaching "them," and the only antecedents for this preposition seem to be "those who were buying and selling," "the money changers," and "those selling doves." He taught them the meaning of the Temple in God's Great Commission plan. He opened to them a way to live differently than they had lived either out of their disobedience or their blindness.

Jesus' work in the lives of the people He corrected can be a model for what He wants to do in your life as this special study ends. Begin now to explore that plan and to pray about it.

1. You probably have been dealing with issues or situations in the past eight weeks that you've known needed your attention for some time. List some of those issues for which you've made intentional and deliberate plans:

_____
_____
_____
_____
_____
_____
_____
_____
_____
_____
_____
_____
_____

2. As you've begun making the needed changes in your life, what has God been able to teach you? Perhaps some truths or insights to which you've been blinded before? List some of the teaching God has provided you:

___

3. Make a prayer list to guide your confession and petition before God in the days and weeks ahead. You'll recognize the categories from other work you've done during this study. Allow God to help you formulate your requests to reflect both top line and bottom line concerns.

Relational concerns:
___

Spiritual concerns:
___

Financial concerns:
___

Physical concerns:
___

Mental concerns:
___

Material concerns:
___

SESSION 8

REWIND

List the seven Old Testament examples given in session 7 that prove the Abrahamic Covenant:
1. _____
2. _____
3. _____
4. _____
5. _____
6. _____
7. _____

Many Old Testament heroes were mentioned in session 7. Beside their names below, jot down a positive characteristic each one possessed that you feel needs to be added to or strengthened in your life.

Abraham: _____
Moses: _____
Solomon: _____
Jeremiah: _____
Nebuchadnezzar: _____
Esther: _____

RECORD

I. Jesus' location of His ministry

  A. Matthew 4:13-16: Jesus lived in _____.
  1. Jews wanted to dispute Jesus as the Messiah because His _____ wasn't in the heart of _____.
  This is A ____ B.
  2. Jesus located His ministry in a mixed _____/_____ area. This is A ____ B.

  B. Matthew 4:24-25: News about Him spread all over _____, and He healed (circle one: some/all/Jews only/Gentiles only) who came to Him.

II. Sending out the twelve and the seventy

  A. Sending out the twelve.
  In Matthew 10:5-8, Jesus said to the twelve disciples, "Go to the lost sheep of Israel." Did Jesus think A was greater than B?
  1. Look at how _____ the disciples were in A > B theology.
  2. Not until Peter's vision of the sheet with clean and unclean animals did the other apostles and believers conclude, "So then, God has granted even the _____ repentance unto life" (Acts 11:18), as if it was totally brand _____.

New Testament Ties to the Abrahamic Covenant

3. What must it have been like in Matthew 10? Even so, he tells them the bottom line: "On my account you will be brought before _____ and _____ as witnesses to them and to the _____" (v.18).

B. Sending out the seventy.
In Luke 10:1-18, Jesus said to the seventy disciples: "The harvest is _____ but the workers are _____."

C. The top line sending was of the _____; the bottom line sending was of the _____.

III. Jesus clearing the Temple

A. Why was Jesus so upset?
1. Outer court was for the _____.
2. The selling and money changing were keeping the Gentiles from _____ _____.

3. At the dedication of the outer court, found in 1 Kings 8:41-43, Solomon prayed that God would answer the foreigner's _____.

B. Jesus was teaching His disciples the bottom line of the covenant. The only gospel writer who caught it, however, was _____, who recorded Jesus as saying, "My house will be called a house of prayer _____ _____ _____" (v. 11:17).

IV. Healing the ten lepers

Read Luke 17:11-19. The only one of the ten who returned to thank Him was a _____.

V. Church persecution

A. God is working an A _____ B strategy to reach the _____.
1. Read Acts 1:8. No _____ is given about where we will be _____.
2. Read Acts 2-7. The gospel is spreading only in _____.
3. Read Acts 8:1. After the stoning of Stephen, believers were scattered to _____ and _____, preaching wherever they went.

B. If you don't do Acts _____, you'll get Acts _____.

C. This is another example of God's _____ go _____.

D. What had kept the believers in Jerusalem?
H _____
J _____
F _____
C _____ E _____
F _____ L _____

Session 8

61

New Testament Ties to the Abrahamic Covenant

1. The stoning of Stephen makes you think A _____ B, because God is willing to persecute His people just to reach the nations.
2. Persecution _____ their walk because they had to _____ only on God.

VI. Is God still in charge of the world's major events?
    A. Kicking out the _____ and putting Khomeini in power in _____

    B. Fall of the _____ _____

    C. Tiananmen Square _____

    D. The falling _____ _____

REPEAT _____

Bob maintains in this final session that some of the best things you can do to strengthen your walk with the Lord are:
1. Get out of your comfort and security.
2. Leave your country.
3. Trust God in ways you've never trusted Him before.

Do any of these suggestions fit with the plans or prayer concerns you listed in PAUSE at the beginning of this session's material? Make some additional notes in the margins.

Bob also offered this challenge: "Most Christians will never know Jesus is all they need until they're put in a place where Jesus is all they have."

Too many Christians have their security in their culture and not in God. This is why God gave the Great Commission. The more you become involved in the bottom line, the more top line you get back.

Answers for the blanks

I. Jesus' location of His ministry
  A. Capernaum
   1. ministry; Judaism; >
   2. Jewish/Gentile; =
  B. Syria; all

II. Sending out the twelve and the seventy
  A.
   1. entrenched
   2. Gentiles; new
   3. governors; kings; Gentiles
  B. plentiful; few
  C. twelve; seventy

III. Jesus clearing the Temple
  A.
   1. Gentiles
   2. worshiping God
   3. prayers
  B. Mark; for all nations

IV. Healing the ten lepers
  Samaritan

V. Church persecution
  A. =; nations
   1. choice; witnesses
   2. Jerusalem
   3. Judea; Samaria
  B. 1:8; 8:1
  C. involuntary; mechanism
  D. What had kept the believers in Jerusalem?
   Homes
   Jobs
   Family
   Children's Education
   Foreign Languages
   1. <
   2. strengthened; rely

VI. Is God still in charge of the world's major events?
  A. missionaries; Iran
  B. Iron Curtain
  C. massacre
  D. Asian economy